{October 45}

JEAN-LOUIS BESSON

{October 45}

CHILDHOOD MEMORIES
OF THE WAR

Translation by Carol Volk
Designed by Rita Marshall

Creative Editions
Harcourt Brace & Company

Foreword

This book is neither the story of the German occupation of Paris, nor that of the Second World War, told for children.

Rather, it is as faithful a recollection as possible of what a little boy in France saw and heard during those years when, contrary to popular belief, most people simply waited for the war to end, taking sides neither for the Resistance nor for collaboration, but rather trying to feed themselves, keep warm, and avoid deprivation as much as possible, simply living through events.

Born to a Catholic family-which is to say neither Jewish nor Communist, a family, therefore, who had nothing to fear from the occupation authorities and for whom order and respect for customs were priorities-a child between the ages of seven and twelve believes just about everything he is told and does not yet pass judgment.

These few memories, however, in no way diminish the fact that for many, the events described here were infinitely more cruel.

Jean-Louis Besson

September 1989. I had just turned seven years old. My family came to Normandy, France, near the town of Deauville, to enjoy our vacation by the sea. The great sandy beach was lined with an endless row of cabins, all of them just sturdy enough to provide shelter on windy days.

That year the most popular song was "Everything's fine, Madame la Marquise!" In the lyrics we heard James, the perfect valet, inform his patroness of her grey mare's death and announce horrifying catastrophes in each verse: The stables burned down, the chateau went up in smoke, and to top it all off, Monsieur le Marquis killed himself. "But aside from that, Madame la Marquise, everything's fine, everything's fine!" went the refrain. We laughed until our sides split.

My parents weren't rich, so during vacations they usually rented half of a small house in the least expensive village on the Normandy coast. There the beach was covered with algae–good for your health because of the iodine it contains, my mother said–and with lots of little bouncing insects we called sea lice. My sister and I liked to race them in the sand...

Among family

This year my family and our two Bengali birds, who constantly flit about their cage, are guests of my Aunt Odette, the richest of my father's sisters. Her husband, my Uncle Eugène, has just built a beautiful villa on top of a hill overlooking the coast.

Though there is talk of war in Poland, everything here is wonderful: the view, the hydrangeas, the two automobiles–even though the larger one, a Talbot, is a little old-fashioned in my opinion. My cousin Jacques, my aunt and uncle's son, is also here. He's eleven years older than me and quite handsome. In the past he and I played with the erector set together, but now elegant young women come to fetch him for rounds of tennis.

And then there are the servants. My aunt says she is always having problems with them: Germaine, the cook, must certainly steal money when she does

her shopping, and her husband, Fernand, the chauffeur, is more often tending to the bottles in the wine cellar than to polishing the cars in the garage. When Aunt Odette goes shopping in Paris, she says, she has to search the neighborhood cafés to find her chauffeur. She doubts whether several apéritifs are good for his driving. Fernand claims that, on the contrary, they help him keep his eyes open to see the road.

The end of our vacation

September 3. It's war!

England and France have declared war on Germany. Uncle Eugène just heard the news on the TSF (that's what we call the wireless, or radio).

Everyone in the house is upset. War- I've been hearing about it for a long time now. Everyone's been very afraid of it, but they hoped that after the big war in 1914, which left millions dead, there would never be another. This is not to be. My father and Uncle Eugène agree that we can't let Hitler, Germany's leader, keep invading neighboring countries-our allies- and do nothing about it. Fortunately, there's the Maginot line! It's a formidable barricade that the French constructed all along their German border. The Germans won't be able to invade France like the last time!

In the meantime, vacation is over. Papa will have to be a soldier; so will Fernand the chauffeur, whose wife is very worried. Mother is even more worried-she always tells us about her three brothers who left for the front in 1914 and returned four years later, grateful to still be alive. But

what about Uncle Eugène, who is too old to be mobilized, and what about us, where should we go? Paris will soon be attacked by German planes! One of mother's brothers, Uncle Albert, lives in Brittany. We decide to go to his house with our birds. Aunt Odette, Uncle Eugène, and my cousin have no family outside of Paris and are happy to come with us. We'll go by train and they'll take the Peugeot 202, because the big Talbot would consume too much gasoline.

My cousin Jacques is the only one happy about the idea of a journey. He just got his driver's license and will finally be able to take the wheel! His parents don't know how to drive, so they'll have to trust him now since they no longer have a chauffeur.

Uncle Albert's

Our voyage from Normandy to Brittany is not very pleasant. Crowds of people are squeezed onto the platform at La Chapelle-Anthenaise, a small transfer station, awaiting trains amid hastily packed luggage. Many of the railroad employees have already left to join their regiments, like Papa, and things are very disorganized. With every sputtering puff of smoke we think our train has arrived, but it's never the right one.

Night falls. Mother is nervous and Papa is no longer here to reassure her. My sister, who is four years older than I am, is trying to calm her down. The birds are no longer flitting about their cage under the cover; they must have fallen asleep. I must have done the same.

Our train finally arrives with a great clamor of push rods and

pistons. It is packed with travelers, who are crammed into the corridors and compartments.

Early in the morning we arrive in Vitré, a small Breton city far from the sea, where Uncle Albert runs a store that sells and repairs bicycles and sewing machines. We are happy to see cousin Yvette and her younger brother, whom we call Bébert (to tell him apart from his father, who has the same first name), and their dog, Rip. He's a rat terrier, but he attacks cats more than rats, probably because he sees them more often.

Best of all, Aunt Reine is here; she's a wonderful cook who likes everyone around her to eat well. Her specialties are veal's head with vinaigrette, pike with butter, and rabbit stew.

Settling in

Aunt Reine quickly found us a place to live: two rooms in a brand new clinic, which we can rent because there aren't any patients yet–no one can afford to go there because of the war. The director of the clinic, a doctor, is at least a captain or a commanding officer. He has an exquisite uniform: a red velvet cap, a sword belt, and leather boots. He also has a wife; a mother-in-law with a big red nose (she always has a bottle of wine in her grocery bag); two daughters, Monique and Colette, whom my sister Geneviève and I will be able to play with; and Jim, a big yellow dog with pointed ears who frightens me, even though they assure me he doesn't bite.

Three days later Uncle Eugène, Aunt Odette, and cousin Jacques arrive in their little Peugeot. They move into the Evergreen Oak Hotel, the fanciest in town. But nothing happens in terms of the war–Hitler is afraid of the French army, says Uncle Eugène–and after a week their family decides to go back to Paris.

After a few weeks Papa gets a leave to spend a week with us. It's the first time I've ever seen him dressed as a soldier, but his uniform is not as nice as the doctor's. Papa tells us that he'd already worn a soldier's uniform, during the First World War, in "horizon blue," the color the French had chosen as camouflage to blend in with the color of the sky, rather than the khaki worn by the other armies. Instead of boots he wears long bands of fabric, called puttees, wrapped around his calves. If the pin that holds the bands in place opens, it all unravels.

Since he joined the artillery, Papa has been making shells for cannons in Pamiers, which is close to Toulouse, in the south of France. It's far from the Maginot line, but Mother still doesn't feel comfortable about it because of all the gunpowder stored there that could explode.

When the leave is up, Papa returns to his factory. He writes that he is not making many shells because the work is so badly organized. They have the powder, but the rest of the parts are missing. There's nothing to do for fun, either. To avoid boredom, he and his friends go to the country to gather snails. They bring them back to the cook to liven up the usual fare.

Daily life

We've been in Vitré for quite a while now. Mother found a job at the post office. She sits behind a counter, weighing packages and sticking on stamps. Everyone in town knows her and everyone likes her. My sister, Geneviève, is enrolled in the same school as Yvette, and I'm attending the boys' school with my cousin Bébert.

My uncle has sold lots of bicycles, and there are fewer and fewer bicycles left in his store. People think that a bicycle will always come in handy—in fact, those who have cars are beginning to hide them under piles of blankets in their garages so they won't be requisitioned by the military.

Behind the store, way in the back near a tiny garden with chickens and rabbits, there's a workshop with a big electric motor, pulleys, and belts. It smells good—of gasoline and paint. Here Uncle Albert and his

partner Maurice fix anything that rolls on two wheels.

On the roof of the workshop is a pigeon house. Uncle Albert returned from the war of 1914 with a love of homing pigeons. They're birds specially trained to always return to their homes, even if they are set loose very far away. My uncle says that during the war of 1870, they served France by transporting messages tied to their feet in a little container. Uncle Albert is very proud of his pigeons, who are known to the whole town of Vitré. Every Sunday at noon he opens the windows of the pigeon house, and the birds–there are at least fifty of them–fly high up in the sky and circle the city before swooping back down and returning home.

Sometimes Uncle Albert climbs on the roof with a little pistol and shoots two or three of them, for the kitchen. He tells me that he always chooses the weakest ones and that if we didn't eat a few from time to time, soon there would be too many of them.

At school, my classmates laugh at my accent, which they think is very Parisian. I think that they're the ones who talk funny, but there are too many of them to mock. Their accent seems as strange to me as their behavior in church on Sundays, when almost everyone remains standing near the door. Yvette says it's so they can get out quickly once Mass is over.

On the outskirts of the city, English soldiers are camping in an old barracks and in tents. We like to go say hello to them after school, especially when they roast chestnuts. They have funny helmets, almost as flat as plates. They wear them cocked over one eye, which doesn't protect the

other side of their heads and seems dangerous to me. They don't really speak French, and we certainly don't speak English, but they manage to teach us to sing a cheery march called "It's a Long Way to Tipperary." We teach them "Nous irons pendre notre linge sur la ligne Siegfried" (We'll hang our laundry on the Siegfried line), the latest hit of the Ray Ventura orchestra, the same orchestra that played "Everything's fine, Madame la Marquise."

The Siegfried line is like the Maginot line, but it was built by the Germans on their side of the border. Everyone says it's not as good.

The phony war

Between the store and the workshop is a big room that Aunt Reine uses as a café, serving cider to the clients waiting for their bicycles or motorbikes to be repaired. When his work is finished, Uncle Albert often drinks a bowl of cider himself and discusses the events at hand.

In fact, nothing is happening. The newspapers are calling it "the phony war" because no one is fighting. The English and the French don't want to start anything until the Germans attack.

So Uncle Albert recounts his memories of World War I, the "big" war, the one that was fought in muddy trenches for over four years. He tells how one day he had to kill a Kraut (that's what they call the Germans to show they don't like them) who suddenly appeared right in front of him, from around the corner of a house. If Uncle Albert hadn't shot first, he would have been the dead one. When he opened the German's wallet, he saw photographs and letters like the ones he had from his own family.

Uncle Albert is always a little upset when he tells this story. But he's still very proud of the military cross and the medal he was given for having fought well.

Distrust

We're afraid of spies; we think they're everywhere. On the walls are posters that say, "Careful, be quiet! The walls have ears!" There are people who might be listening to everything we say and telling the enemy. They are part of the invisible "fifth column," made up of ordinary-looking people who send messages to the other side, to the enemy army.

One afternoon, when the street is quiet, a motorcyclist stops in front of the store to buy gasoline, which Aunt Reine sells in drums in addition to running the café. The man hardly speaks. His clothing resembles a uniform but isn't one. His helmet is strange, and his motorcycle has no manufacturer's name on it.

Aunt Reine runs to get my uncle. "Albert, come quickly. Take a look!" she calls.

The neighbors and passersby approach. "We've never seen him—he's not from around here," they whisper. "He may not be French! Quick—someone should ask him the time in German to see if he responds; that's how they catch spies. He must surely be from the fifth column!"

The motorcyclist still doesn't speak.

Uncle Albert introduces himself: "Chief War-
rant Officer Bonnaffoux, second regiment of reserve
alpine riflemen. Show me your papers!" It turns out
that the man's identity card and driver's license are, in
fact, in order. He lives a bit farther along. He's tired and
doesn't feel like talking. His clothing and motorcycle
are covered with dust and mud.

The collapse

Every day cars pass through town on their way from Paris or from the east of France. The cars have mattresses, tables, and chairs tied to their roofs and entire families crowded inside. The Germans have entered France. The Maginot line didn't stop them; they went around it, by way of the Belgian border. But the refugees think they may not advance all the way to Brittany.

At the same time, we watch as the English soldiers leave town. There are too many Germans for them to fight. They make a last round of Vitré, singing in their trucks. Later we read in the paper that they were heading toward the coast, where ships came to take them home to regroup.

England's new prime minister, Winston Churchill, has vowed to continue fighting.

The invasion

June. The Germans are here! No one thought they
would arrive so quickly. The war is no longer a phony
war. Tears stream down Uncle Albert's face as he

watches the Germans pass in front of the store, in perfect formation, on
their motorbikes and in their trucks. He says, "When I think how hard we
fought during the other war...We would never have let them get this far!"

The beginning of the occupation

Two German officers visited the doctor today to ask permission to stay in his house-only in the guest room, so as not to bother anyone. They speak French very well. The doctor says they're very proper, for enemies.

At Uncle Albert's, Miss Leduby, the grocer, tells us that a German soldier came into her store this morning. This one didn't speak French, but when he pointed to a jar sitting on the counter, she understood that he wanted one of the wrapped confections that were inside. Since he didn't have any money to pay, she gave it to him. He unwrapped the gold paper, put the confection in his mouth and immediately started yelling "Oh! Oh!"

in German before running out of the store. It was a
concentrated bouillon cube, which made us all laugh.
But everyone agrees that the German soldiers seem
well disciplined. We certainly won't be finding them
on the streets at night making a drunken racket like
the English.

Two weeks later we see Papa way at the end of the
road that leads to the clinic. He's carrying a little suit-
case in his hand. We've been worried about him; we've
had no news from him because the mail isn't operat-
ing. He traveled any way he could from Pamiers-
hitchhiking, on carts, by train sometimes, and often on
foot. His shoes have holes in them. He no longer has
socks, but the puttees held up. For him the war is over.
France has asked for an armistice. In other words, our
country has promised not to fight anymore. We're so
happy to have Papa back with us!

Life begins again

It's summer again and school is out. The rural police passed through the streets today and, after a drum roll, informed the population that all orders would now be coming from the German kommandantur, now located next to the town hall in the old castle of the city. The first order: curfew at 9:00 p.m. Everyone must go home, and all lights must be out. As for Uncle Albert's pigeons, they are no longer allowed to fly over the city, probably for fear they'll transport secret messages. At least they weren't confiscated.

Uncle Albert now travels by bicycle to farmers' homes to repair the separators, the machines that separate the cream from the milk and make butter. Many people are also bringing him sewing machines now, since there are rarely any new clothes in the stores. Aunt Reine still serves cider in her café, and Mama, behind her counter, still sends letters and packages, sometimes to Germany for the prisoners.

My father had to look for a job. Before the war he'd worked at home. He drew postcards and posters for the Boy Scouts. He also painted decorations on the silk stoles worn by priests for important ceremonies. Best of all, he had just finished a book, *Annecy, Flower of the Mountains*, about a lake in Savoy that he likes very much. He had done everything–the text,

the photographs, and the drawings. Now, however, he is an "Economic Regulation Inspector." He visits the merchants to check that their scales are accurate; if they're not he gives a summons. My aunt and uncle aren't very happy about this because many of their friends are merchants.

My cousin Bébert gave me a little bicycle he once used. I might never have learned to ride a bicycle if I had stayed in Paris. When he finishes helping his father in the workshop, we go for rides. Rip follows us, his ears flapping in the wind and his tongue hanging out.

The return to Paris

September. Since France is no longer fighting with Germany, my father decided we should return to Paris to our apartment, which is in the Belleville section, near the Buttes Chaumont Park, where I used to ride the merry-go-round.

As soon as we get home, Mama removes the covers she'd placed on the armchairs before we left for vacation last year. My sister and I return to our rooms; the erector set and the electric train are still in their boxes under my bed. I imagine that our Bengali birds are happy to be back in their spot in front of the dining room window. Our gas masks are still in their steel boxes in the broom closet. I remember the day we went to the town hall to pick them up. They had been handed out to everyone in the neighborhood at the first threat of war. The canvas-and-rubber masks all smelled bad and  made people look like insects. When I tried mine on I thought I was going to suffocate. I really hope we'll never have to use them.

We also return to our parish–the St. Jean-Baptiste-de-Belleville Church is at the end of our street, with the priest and all his abbots. I resume my place in the children's choir during Mass on Sunday, wearing a white surplice and red soutane. My sister and I also go back to the parish school, the girls' school and the boys'. Every day we exit in rows, two by two, the little ones in front and the taller ones behind.

My father has to look for work again. He would like to be able to make other books, but that is no longer possible. In the meantime, he has no choice but to accept the offer made by Uncle Gaston, his sister Amelia's husband, to work in his factory in Montreuil.

Every morning when I get up for school, I catch a glimpse of my father on his way out, dressed in a blue worker's outfit, his lunch satchel slung over his shoulder.

First alert

One night, after we'd been asleep for a long time, the sirens started blaring. They are positioned nearby, on top of the water tanks on the rue du Télégraphe (the highest spot in Paris, a meter higher than the hill of Montmartre, a fact of which the neighborhood is very proud). We had heard the sirens scream before, but it was only a test to see if they worked. Tonight it means that airplanes really are going to bomb Paris.

It is four in the morning. We put on our coats and go down to the subway for shelter. Our station is one of the deepest in Paris, and my father often says that it's a much safer place than the basement of our building, which could crumble and bury us if a bomb were to fall on it.

Everyone in the neighborhood is here. Many have come with folding stools, blankets, and thermoses. Their nightshirts and pajamas are sticking out of their coats. A lot of the women knit. Some people play cards. I find my friends Naudinat and Desrumeaux, who suggest we go walking on the rails since the electric current is turned off. Why not go through the tunnel all the way to the next station? We'll surely find other friends there. Seen from the track, the tunnel looks tall and scary; we can barely see and we keep twisting our ankles on the stones between the ties. What if the alert ends and the current comes back on? "They'd blow

some whistles to warn us!" Naudinat, the oldest, assures us. But as the lights of the Pyrénées station become barely visible we decide to turn around.

The next day we learn that it was the Renault factories in Billancourt that had been targeted. A bomb even entered a neighboring house

through the stairwell and exploded in

the basement, killing the people who thought they were protected there.

My father says that the metro is definitely the safest shelter.

Marshal, here we are!

Marshal Pétain has been our new head of state since July. He is a former World War I hero and is supposed to be France's savior, as it says in the song that we learned in school that begins "Marshal, here we are!" We see his photograph everywhere, at school and in store windows. After school, we are asked to sell postcards with his portrait that say "I gave myself to France." We sell them on the street and collect the money in metal boxes marked "National Relief" to help the poor and the elderly.

At school we are also given cookies and candy with vitamins, to fortify us. Unfortunately the cookies have no chocolate, and the candies are pink lozenges with a funny taste.

One Thursday a big festival is held at the Winter Stadium for all the schoolchildren in Paris. The singer Fréhel, a very fat lady dressed

in blue, white, and red, makes us sing "Marshal, Here We Are!" again. We also sing "Up There on the Mountain," another song we learned at school that tells how Jean, a young shepherd, saw his old worm-eaten chalet carried away by gusts of wind. So "Jean, with his valiant heart, reconstructed it better than before," just as they tell us we now have to do for France.

They talk to us a lot about mountains and pure air. My sister is reading a very popular novel called *First on the Rope*. She tells me it's the story of a guide from Savoy who is attracted to the highest summits and the invigorating air one breathes there. Unfortunately the book ends badly—the guide dies, struck down during a storm, and remains frozen like a statue, way up on top of his mountain.

Ask forgiveness

The priest tells us that we should pray for forgiveness. France has committed many sins. Fortunately we can turn to the Blessed Virgin, for France was put under her special protection. She will no doubt ask her son, our Lord, to pardon and save the French. In fact the Blessed Virgin has always loved France, which is why she chose the town of Lourdes in which to appear and bring about famous miracles. And who is in a better position than a mother to convince her son?

At night my mother often makes me and my sister recite a prayer in which we say, "And groaning under the weight of my sins." My mother really likes this prayer, but I find it a bit extreme.

At catechism my sister and I are among the Crusaders, a youth group. Every week we have to fill out a report called a treasure, making marks in two columns, one for sins and the other for good deeds. On Thursdays we hand them in to our "zealot," who is an older student. The sins are often easy to think of, like saying curse words, lying, or getting angry. The other column is more complicated. You can't find a blind person to help across the street every day. So my sister and I consider that going to get the bread when Mother asks us to counts as a good action, and we always have one or two marks in the good column.

An exhibition

Of course, not everyone believes in God. Not counting those who are lazy and prefer to stay in bed on Sundays instead of going to Mass, there are the Communists, the Freemasons and the Jews. The Communists are atheists; people claim that the Freemasons dare to walk on crucifixes during their secret ceremonies; and as for the Jews, they refuse to recognize Jesus Christ as the true Messiah. It seems all these people are responsible for France's troubles.

In Paris, in fact, there is an exhibition on the main boulevards entitled "The Jew and France" that teaches us how to recognize Jews, because we have to be careful of them. They have big hooked noses, they're not very clean, and they only think about making money. Our teacher offers to take us to the exhibition, since school children are particularly welcome and are admitted free on Thursdays. But my parents think it's not a subject for children and I don't go.

Small posters have appeared in the windows of certain stores that say "Jewish Establishment." You see them often in the windows of the many clothing and shoe stores in Belleville. This is, no doubt, to tell us to avoid going there. Of course we don't pay any attention. We know all the shopkeepers in our neighborhood and we like them. In any case, there is less and less merchandise for sale, and everyone says it's not good quality.

These days, most shoes have wooden soles that clatter when you walk. Others have cork or split plywood soles that bend, but everyone says they're not sturdy. Uncle Gaston gives us an old tire from his car, which my father cuts into pieces to nail to the bottoms of our shoes. It makes the soles stronger.

The ladies complain that they can't buy any stockings. My three cousins in Montreuil, who are very elegant, tint their legs with walnut stain from the paint store and then draw false seams on them with a pencil. They say that all their friends do the same. It's very pretty, but of course it doesn't keep them warm.

People are having trouble finding clothes, and yet sometimes you see strange young people, the zazous, who have started a new style of wearing incredible outfits. Jackets that are way too big over short, narrow trousers, ties as narrow as strings, hats pushed back and shoes with enormous soles. They always have umbrellas in their hands, especially when the weather is nice. The girls have bouffant hairdos, enormous hats, and skirts that don't even reach their knees.

Supplies

The main problem we face is finding food. In the German system you need tickets to buy everything. Everyone has a food card, with different categories depending on one's age, from J1 for babies to V for the elderly. My sister and I are J2, which gives us the right to more bread, milk, and meat than the adults. When we reach sixteen we'll be J3, unless of course the war ends before then.

We are constantly waiting in line at the stores, especially if they sell products that don't require tickets, like leeks or potatoes. Often the wait is very long and Mother asks us to stand in line for her. The folding chair has become a necessity. One thing you can always buy, though, is rutabagas. You don't need a ticket and you don't have to wait in line to buy them, either, because they're not very good. They're big turnips that are ordi-

narily used to feed animals in the country.

We've found that you can make all sorts of dishes with potatoes, even cake if you have a little flour. Instead of coffee we grill barley. We call that an ersatz, which is a German word that means substitute. Tobacco is also rationed and smokers make cigarettes out of mint or eucalyptus leaves, or with flower petals. But no one in our house smokes.

There is also the black market. You can buy anything there if you have the money. My friend Pignel, the son of the eyeglass merchant, tells me that every week his parents buy a big fat steak. It's expensive, of course, but very good. Aunt Odette has a friend, Mr. Peyronnet, who works at police headquarters with the Germans and who brings her gifts from time to time–a bottle of oil or a leg of lamb–hidden in a newspaper. She speaks of him in a hushed voice.

Fortunately, Aunt Reine, who still lives in Vitré, never fails to send us a package whenever she can. She always includes a chicken or rabbit, butter, and lard. Enough to get by. From time to time, we also get a pigeon.

In the summer, on Sundays when the weather is good, we take the train to the country with all our picnic baskets and gather mulberries in the bushes. They make a good inexpensive dessert for no tickets. We could also gather mushrooms, but my parents say it's too dangerous, that we might pick the wrong ones and get a stomachache, or worse . . .

Family life

My father no longer works at the factory in Montreuil. He went back to his profession as an illustrator, or almost. Now he teaches drawing at fashionable schools in fancy neighborhoods. Some of his students are from famous French families~with names like Murat, de Broglie, de Dampierre~but that doesn't necessarily make them good at respecting the laws of perspective, which my father is very finicky about. At night, when he brings their exercises home to correct, we push aside the chairs and place the drawings on the rug. The entire class always works on the same subject, a vase with flowers or apples on a plate drawing, or else-the most important exercise, which every student must tackle at least once during the year-a landscape with a street corner, a house and a tree. Everyone in the family gives an opinion, judging the placement of the vanishing point and the horizon line, and also the colors. The bad drawings, however, are usually the most fun to look at.

On holidays, Papa sits down at the piano. He carefully lifts the keyboard cover, removes the long silk band that protects the ivory keys, adjusts the height of the stool, and plays us Mozart's "Turkish March" or Mendelssohn's "Springtime," his favorite tunes. To conclude, we always ask him to play "Invitation to the Waltz," my mother's favorite song.

In addition to preparing three meals a day, doing the housekeeping, and waiting in line at the shops, my mother goes around to bookstores to sell *Annecy, Flower of the Mountains*, Papa's book. We still have several thousand of them, arranged in rows of twelve along the wall of the room that looks onto the courtyard, the same room where my father keeps his photography equipment and where he transforms tires into soles for shoes. My mother also takes the books to the post office to send out orders. She says they're heavy to carry.

My sister would like to be a dancer at the Opera. She keeps a box with signed photographs of star dancers, especially Yvette Chauviré, her favorite. She also bought pink shoes. On the afternoons when we don't have school, I hear my sister and her friend, Josette, who also loves dance, practice walking on their toes across the living room.

Once a week we go to the movies. There are three theaters right nearby, the Fairyland, the Alcazar, and the Florida, as well as the Folies-Belleville and the Ménil-Palace a little farther away. They all change shows every Wednesday. Many of the films take place in the last century, like *Les Miserables, The Count of Monte-Cristo,* or *Pontcarral, Colonel of the Empire.* Some take place around 1900, like *The Marriage of Chiffon,* in the days of parasols and the first cars that backfired and shook their passengers—which always makes us laugh. The beautiful costumes and the candlelight parties are a nice change from wooden shoe soles and ration tickets.

We finally have a wireless set at home. My father had always refused to buy one, saying that it was too expensive and that all you heard was garbage, but now we need to listen to the English broadcast like everyone else. It's forbidden by the government, of course, and we have to adjust the sound very low, just as everyone else does, because of neighbors who might turn us in.

Every evening the program begins with four slightly mysterious, muffled sounds: "Boom, boom, boom, boom," and then, "From London, the French speak to the French." You really have to make an effort to listen

because of the static, and also because the program disappears completely at certain moments. They say that the war is far from over and that
the Germans will end up losing. And there's a French general in London
whom no one has ever heard of~General de Gaulle~who is calling on people to continue to fight on the side of the English. But here no one really
believes that together  we could win the war.

Paris by night

At night the city turns completely black. According to the curfew, as soon
as evening falls, no light may shine from any house, not even the slightest
glow from the edge of a curtain. The cracks in the shutters have all been
plugged up with newspapers or pieces of rag. The lamps are covered with
blue paint that is just barely transparent, as are the headlights of the few

cars. With bicycles and cars it's all right to leave a narrow crack to let a
little light shine through.

    This doesn't stop anyone from visiting friends. All you have to do

is carry a flashlight, also painted blue, quickly turning it on in case you encounter an obstacle, and return home before eleven to avoid running into the booted steps of a patrol.

A perilous return to school

October. I've finished primary school and am now entering the fifth grade at Voltaire High School. My sister will continue to attend the parish school until she gets her certificate. She is also learning to sew and to play the piano. My father says that's fine for a girl, but for boys it's different. We have to get our high school diplomas and finish our studies at a major university. My parents already see me going to the engineering school, since I like playing with the erector set, and maybe even to the Polytechnic, a famous engineering college.

Father Ledeur, our chaplain, often warned us how hard it would be for me and my friends to switch to the public school and to be among so many people without religion. He even compared us to the first Christians who were thrown into the lions' den in Rome, like St. Blandine, who preferred to be trampled by a mad bull rather than deny her faith. We too would need great courage; we would have to pray and make our guardian angels proud of us.

The first day back to school I expect the worst. But nothing happens. The general supervisor even stops by our class and asks very respectfully for the names of those who would like to enroll in catechism. Only the history professor worries me. According to him, the Flood, Noah's Ark, and the crossing of the Red Sea are just old legends inspired by cataclysms and tidal waves that shook the earth a long time ago. I say nothing, but I think I hear the rustling of my guardian angel's feathers . . .

Practically the entire class chooses German for a foreign language. The general opinion is that one must, unfortunately, learn to keep up with the times. Two students nonetheless raise their hands: They want to learn English. Everyone wonders what good it will do them.

Our singing teacher, Miss Merleau, is dressed in green from head to toe. The German uniforms are green, too, so we've nicknamed her "Fräulein Grün," which is Miss Green in German. Fräulein Grün wants to teach us the hunter's chorus of Weber's *Freischütz*. She says it's a manly song and that we should model ourselves on the Germans who sing so well in chorus. We make an enormous racket, singing and stamping our feet to sound even more warlike.

On the way to high school

The advantage of High School over grammar school is that it's a half an hour walk from home and that means a long walk through new streets. Along the way I always run into friends~Loiseau, Hardy or Gourgues, who's very proud because his father is a tenor at the Opera.

In the morning, the delivery horses eat their oats and stomp their hooves while the sparrows hover around the manure. Women in slippers with coats over their nightgowns are running their first errands. It's also the time when automobile drivers poke their gas generators, strange

stoves that make gas out of wood to replace gasoline. It doesn't smell very good and doesn't work
as well, especially uphill.

At night, we have plenty of time to stop in
front of the cinemas on our way
home. They're closed, but the smell
of the theaters and their plush seats
comes through the gates and makes
me dream that the show is about to
begin. We look at the pictures, especially the ones of films we aren't
allowed to see, the ones with actresses who wear lots
of lipstick and draw their eyebrows with a pencil.
This provokes discussions as to women's many
hidden peculiarities, which are always very
mysterious.

The Germans have no shortage of gasoline for their cars but they also walk a
great deal because they seem to like Paris.
At every intersection they've installed
signposts with big black letters on
white backgrounds, which they must
be able to read from far away. They are
very organized people.

Widespread fighting

Elsewhere the war continues. London is bombed almost every day. Will the English soon have to surrender as well? "England, like Carthage, will be destroyed!" That is what Jean Herold-Paquis, a journalist on Radio-Paris, repeats every night on the air, just as the statesman Cato did in Roman times, according to our Latin teacher.

Hitler attacked Stalin, who was supposed to be his ally, and the Germans entered Russia with their tanks just as easily as they had entered France the year before. Unfortunately they're stronger than anyone else.

"If only the Americans would enter the war, like in 1917, things might change," say my father and my uncles. (My father has four sisters and my mother has three brothers, so I have a lot of aunts, uncles, and cousins.) At the end of the year, in fact, the Japanese launch a surprise attack on the American flotilla at Pearl Harbor, on the Hawaiian Islands in the Pacific Ocean, and declare war on the United States. Since the Germans are allied with the Japanese, they too declare war on the Americans. Now it's a World War. The radio in London assures us that it's the beginning of defeat for the Germans.

Our cousins from Versailles are lucky enough to live in their own house. They proudly show us a ping-pong table in their attic that they transformed into a global battlefield. Armies, tanks, and planes are represented by little pieces of painted wood decorated with rosettes or swastikas. The naval battles are the most impressive part, and the armored ships, with their chimneys and cannon turrets, look absolutely real.

Winter has arrived. It's very cold. It snows a great deal, and the windows are covered with frost in leafy patterns. To keep warm we use balls
made of the compressed dust of low-grade coal, which we burn in the big
furnace in the kitchen, where the four of us huddle together. At night my
mother warms the beds with a brick heated in the oven and wrapped in
a rag. Once in bed we mustn't move, if we want to stay warm.

The yellow star

"Work, Family, Nation" is France's new motto, replacing the old "Liberty, Equality, Fraternity." Everyone talks about working in communion with the earth. To be a farmer is a beautiful profession that should inspire young people, who can serve France by living in the country, far from the factories and cafés. Being an artisan is also a beautiful profession. Carpenters, potters, and shoemakers should be our models: work with one's hands to rebuild France. "The French should no longer be concerned about the war," says Marshal Pétain.

This is not what the people in the Resistance, who attack German soldiers by surprise and derail trains, think. The newspapers say they are terrorists and saboteurs. After each attack the Germans arrest people from the general population and warn that they will be shot in revenge. Posters on the walls announce the death of hostages or show photos of wanted terrorists, who are often accused of being Jews or Communists to boot.

Since spring, Jews have had to wear yellow stars sewn on their clothing, inscribed with the word "Jew." Several students have them in my class at school, near the collar of their jackets and on their

coats. It turns out Miss Rosenthal, who comes to the
house every Thursday to give my sister piano lessons,
is Jewish. You can barely see her star, which is half
covered by the long fur of her coat, which she never
takes off. She's pretty nice, even though she frightens
my sister a little when she reprimands her for playing
the wrong notes.

The big roundup

July. It's the beginning of summer vacation. This morning, as usual, the entire family is in the kitchen for breakfast. My mother is pale and seems very upset. At five in the morning she was awakened by a hard rapping on a door and cries of "Police, open up!" and by the sound of sobbing. She couldn't get back to sleep and is surprised we didn't hear anything. It came from the courtyard, where some poor families live. A little later, leaning out the window, she saw policemen forcing people onto a bus. We learned that all the Jews who lived in Belleville, our neighborhood, were arrested and assembled at the Winter Stadium before being taken somewhere else—we don't know where.

In the back of the courtyards behind the buildings, there are many leather workshops and shoe manufacturers, many of which belong to Jews. Leather is a neighborhood specialty. Today, however, everything is quiet.

The priest comes to visit us, as he does from time to time with his most faithful parishioners. He speaks to us again about the Blessed Virgin, to whom we must pray more than ever, since, as we know, she loves France especially. In fact, it is thanks to her protection that the French are not suffering so much at the hands of the Germans, who are tolerable enemies after all, and Christians like us. We get on our knees and the priest blesses us in Latin, in a hushed voice, his head bent slightly.

As he nears the door to leave, my mother says: "But Father, you say that the Germans behave well, and yet what they did to the Jews, arresting entire families

and taking them away to work camps probably, isn't good. It's horrible. I think about it every day."

"Oh, Mrs. Besson," the priest replies, "the Jews allowed Jesus to be condemned on the cross! And now, what do you expect, they've got troubles."

Vacation

My sister and I return to Vitré for vacation. We're lucky to have family in Brittany. Many of my friends stay in Paris all summer.

There are still German officers at the doctor's house, but not the same ones. People say that the new ones don't speak French and are far less civil. They occupy not only the guest room but the entire house. The doctor, his wife, and his two daughters had to move into the rooms set aside for the sick, the ones we had rented two years ago.

Now that I can ride a big bicycle, I accompany Uncle Albert when he goes to the farms to fix the separators. We take the tandem, a bicycle for two that goes much faster. Uncle Albert steers and I just pedal. The roads are lined with hedges and with all kinds of trees. When we reach the last turn we finally see the farm, just as the stable smells grow stronger and the first chickens scurry into the thickets. Our arrival in the courtyard always provokes a loud concert from the ducks, dogs, and pigs.

There is no electricity in the country, and the separators are operated by a crank. My uncle takes them apart. I help him by putting the nuts and screws on a table and watching them, because they tend to roll on the floor. He often whispers that all the machine needed was a good cleaning, that dried milk was blocking the works.

When we're finished working, the farmers invite us into the common room, with its packed earth floor, its big chimney, and beds in each corner. We all drink cider out of the same bowl. Uncle Albert drinks first, then everyone else takes a sip. I drink last, since I'm the youngest. We talk about the events at hand and about the fact that the Germans collect all the farm products. Fortunately everyone man-

ages to keep something back, and my uncle always takes home a block of butter or a chicken hidden under the tools in the bicycle's satchel.

At night, when the store closes, we listen to the English broadcast the BBC. The programs are always jammed by the Germans with a three-note whistle, but we still manage to hear the news. Ever since they invaded Russia it seems as if the Germans have given up bombing London. Maybe they're having trouble being everywhere at once. The moment we all anticipate is the one when coded messages are broadcast. We pay close attention, as if the messages are meant for us. My uncle says that they announce very important things, weapons deliveries or perhaps even the arrival of parachutists. "The wolf bit the sheep-twice . . . The sparrows aren't coming this spring . . . The carrots are cooked . . . " We wonder what it all means. But the Resistance fighters must know.

On Sundays the entire family heads out on bicycles to go fishing. Uncle Albert and Aunt Reine go first on the tandem, with the rods and the nets attached to the long frame. Yvette, Bébert, my sister and I follow them as best we can, with Rip sitting, for once, in a basket. There are many ponds near Vitré and the fish are easy to catch.

In the afternoons, when I'm not riding my bicycle with my cousin Bébert, I sit at a table in Aunt Reine's café and draw. War pictures, of course. The English and the Americans are fighting the Germans and are always stronger!

A minute of silence

October. It's time to go back to Voltaire High School. Now I'm in the sixth grade. The day begins with Mr. Baboulène's Latin class. We all know Mr. Baboulène—he's a nice old man, bald with a little white beard. He calls roll. Most of my fellow students from last year are here. Then we have French class and then math, at which I'm not very gifted. This doesn't bode well for getting into the Polytechnical school and makes my father sad.

In the afternoon we meet our history and geography professor. He's new. His name is Guillermin; he's from Toulouse and has a slight south-western accent. "You have probably noticed that some of your fellow students haven't returned," he says. "I'm talking about those who wore yellow stars. You went on vacation, and they also went away. No one can say exactly where they are, of course. Probably far away, in a camp, performing hard labor like breaking rocks to repair roads. They may come back one day, or you may never see them again. No one knows. I ask you to think of them for a moment, you who are lucky enough to be in this class, and close to your families too."

For several moments no one says a word. Then class begins.

Ice and snow

January. This winter seems colder than the last one. Snow and mud are everywhere. But this is nothing compared to the Russian winter that we see on the newsreels in the movie theater. Things aren't going so well for the Germans. For the first time, the snow-covered tanks are caught in the ice. The German divisions aren't advancing. The fighting around Stalingrad is fierce and lasts all winter. Marshal von Paulus, head of the German troops in Russia, is surrounded. He is forced to surrender and is taken prisoner with his entire army! On the other fronts, the Germans are often forced to withdraw. Radio-Paris and the newspapers explain that they are "strategic withdrawals," intended to regroup forces and strengthen the coming attack. But the

London radio plays a song making fun of this: "Ha, ha, ha, ha~It's the elastic retreat! Ha, ha, ha, ha~What could be so sweet!"

Now everyone is talking about the obligatory work service. Men between the ages of twenty~one and twenty~three must go to Germany to work in weapons factories. My cousins in Versailles, Robert and Lucien, the ones with the war map in their attic, aren't all that worried because they already work for the Germans here in Paris, at the printers of *Signal*, the German magazine, and will probably be exempt from the service. But the other men have no choice but to obey or hide. Several young people in our neighborhood disappear. Rumor has it they went to join the Resistance.

Two vocations

One Thursday~catechism day~Father Ledeur interrupts our games and tells us, "My boys, I have important news to tell you, very important news! Let us first kneel and pray . . . Our Father who art in heaven, hallowed be Thy name; Thy kingdom come . . . My children, let us thank the Lord! I would like to announce that the Holy Spirit has descended on one of you, on the head of your fellow student André Schreiber, who has informed me that he suddenly heard the call. I announce to you with great solemnity: our friend Dédé would like to become a priest! We are all very fortunate in this, for now he can pray for us."

André Schreiber is there, on his knees like everyone else, and I try to imagine the white dove that landed on his head, which of course no one can see because the Holy Spirit is invisible. He is ten years old, like me. He's shy and has fat cheeks and blushes easily. His parents have a bakery. He's a good friend but not a very good student. "How will he manage?" my father wants to know. "You have to study to be a priest, at least as far as the baccalaureate."

A few months later, Schreiber comes to see us one Thursday at the youth club. He tells us he has entered the seminary and has been promised he can become a priest thanks to a dispensation, for his vocation is very strong. Four years from now, he could be wearing the black cloth.

Maurice Escudier came to visit my father. To me Escudier is a grown-up. The first year I went to school, he was the one who brought me home at night, since it was also on his way home. He's a good student and a serious boy. My parents are very fond of him. Today he has come to ask advice. He wants to enlist in the French volunteer legion fighting against Bolshevism. My father thinks he's rather young to go to war on the Russian front.

"I'll be seventeen soon, Mr. Besson. I want to fight!"

"Why do you want to fight?"

"Against the Bolsheviks! Communism is the greatest threat Christianity has ever known. It's the work of the Devil."

"But the war is terrible over there, and the Germans are withdrawing."

"That's why we have to fight by their sides, to help them. That's why I want to enlist."

A few months later, one Sunday in church as the bell calls the worshippers to bow in silence, I hear heels clicking and a metallic noise. Turning my head slightly, I catch a glimpse of Escudier on the side near a pillar, saluting with his arm outstretched like the German soldiers. We feel a little funny shaking his hand upon leaving the church. He is wearing a German uniform. Only the beret and the blue badge on the front are different. He is very proud of his revolver and his knife, and he tells us he's leaving the next day for the Eastern front, in Russia.

We never see him again.

A plane falls

For some time we've stopped going down into the metro during alerts. We've gotten used to them and feel we have nothing to fear. The places that are most often targeted by the Allies–the Renault and Citroën car factories, where people are making cars and tanks for the Germans–are far from our home. The bombings almost always take place at night. A few seconds after the sirens, we hear the deep, steady drone of the flying fortresses, along with the first detonations of the German anti-aircraft defense. We see the flares attached to parachutes descend. For a moment it's almost as bright as day. The sky sparkles with thousands of tiny silver papers the airplane has dropped. They say that the detection devices react to all these little spinning metallic strips as if they were so many airplanes. Thus, aiming the anti-aircraft cannons becomes impossible. The next morning the streets are covered with these little twists of paper from America, and my friends and I run to gather them up.

One night the spectacle takes a bad turn. The four of us–my parents, sister and I–are at the window. Amid the explosions of shells from the anti-aircraft cannons, we suddenly see a ball of fire. A plane has been hit. Several flaming pieces descend in a slow zigzag, like dead leaves. "My God!" my father says. "Those poor fellows trapped in there!" I've never seen him so moved.

On the seventh and top floor of our building, where the maids' rooms are located, lives a woman no one knows very well because she doesn't talk much. The neighbors think they've noticed that she has been bringing up more provisions in her shopping basket than usual. They whisper that she's hiding an American aviator.

A few fake tickets

Obtaining supplies isn't getting any easier. Bread is still severely rationed. Jojo, our Belgian neighbor on the second floor, works at Farman's, the aviation factory requisitioned by Messerschmitt, the German plane manufacturer. Jojo brought us a letter "A" made of metal like the printers use, the same A that you see on the food cards for bread. He made it on the sly with his colleagues. Unlike the tickets marked 25 or 50 grams, the value of the A ticket varies according to the month, but it is always at least 200 grams higher.

At night, the entire family gets to work. Mother is best at scratching out the 25-gram inscription with an old, carefully sharpened razor blade. As a young girl she drew road maps at Michelin, the tire and map company, and she still has a taste for meticulous work. My father prints the A, which is the most delicate operation. With oil paint and varnish, he recreates the color of the printer's ink. He also makes a wooden guide so that the A falls in just the right spot and isn't crooked in the middle of the ticket, which would be a total loss. My sister Geneviève and I sometimes do touch-ups with a sharpened color pencil.

We're also the ones who go to the bakery with the modified tickets. My parents believe that children always look more innocent.

"D" Day

The Allies have landed in Normandy!

We learned the news on the wireless upon waking this morning-news we'd been awaiting for so long and that never seemed to come. The landing took place on beaches we know very well, like the one in Bernières, where we used to race the jumping sea lice.

I gulp down my chicory with milk and run more than walk the streets to school. I'm anxious to talk about the event with my friends. There's fighting in France now, only 300 kilometers from Paris! Everyone is very excited except for the professors, who do their best to remain impassive-all except Mr. Guillermin, who seems to be smiling. Fräulein Grün looks stern.

That night at home we wait impatiently for the eight o'clock broadcast from London. We learn that the landing had been planned for a long time, but that the secret had been well kept. The Germans were watching the wrong part of the coast and were caught off guard. The fighting is fierce. Many people are dead, and German reinforcements will soon arrive. But the English, Canadians, and Americans are going to hold on at any cost.

Of course, Radio-Paris says exactly the opposite, that the Atlantic wall is impassable and that the assailants will be rapidly cast back to sea. It's true that the concrete blockhouses the Germans have built all along the coasts are formidable, but so must be the bombings in order to destroy them.

My father decided to pin a Michelin map of Normandy to the wall, next to the wireless set. We place thumbtacks everywhere the allied armies have landed and wait until we can stretch a string across to represent the front line.

A murder

July. Philippe Henriot, an editorialist on Radio-Paris, was executed by the French Resistance: Two phony policemen arrived at his house at daybreak and shot him. Philippe Henriot spoke in a nice deep voice on Radio-Paris every evening at a quarter to eight, just before the BBC broadcast. It was our habit to listen to the two stations exchange opposing arguments from either side of the channel. Philippe Henriot would say that if the Americans and the English loved the French as they claimed, they wouldn't destroy the villages and towns of Normandy by bombarding them and killing their inhabitants. The journalists in London responded that the Allies were doing their best to spare the civilian populations and that Henriot was a traitor. Some people were beginning to believe that Philippe Henriot wasn't entirely wrong.

Many people are shocked by his assassination. My father says that no one has the right to kill a person to prevent him from expressing his opinion. Our entire family goes to the Ministry of Information, where Philippe Henriot's body is on view. A large crowd is waiting in silence on the sidewalk. Inside, everyone walks slowly through a room fully draped in black curtains. There are candles and many flowers. It's the first time I've seen a dead man. His face is all white and his black, polished shoes point toward the ceiling.

The last cinema

It's summer again, but this year there is no talk of going away. On the map, the string representing the line of fighting gets closer to Paris every day. The weather is nice and very warm. Certain things are starting to be seriously lacking because the war is so close to Paris. There is electricity only a few hours at night, and the gas pressure has gotten so low we can't cook anymore. The metro and the buses no longer run. But still it's vacation and one has to keep busy. My friend Naudinat read in the newspaper that there was still one-and only one-cinema left open in Paris, the Pathé-Louxor. It's on the boulevard Barbès, which is a bit far, at least an hour's stroll. We decide to go.

The streets are quiet; there is no longer any traffic and most of the
stores are closed. We see almost no one. The inside of the theater is just as
empty. The film is called *Graine au Vent (Seed in the Wind)*. It's the story
of an unruly young girl who becomes a truant. Her father started drinking because his wife left him. But at the end of the film, the little girl, who
isn't so bad after all, manages to convince her father that drinking is bad
and gets him back on the right path.

The Germans go home

August. The Allies are now in Rambouillet, right near Paris. The radio has stopped broadcasting and there are no longer any newspapers. We hear that Jean Hérold-Paquis, the announcer who had predicted the destruction of England every night on Radio-Paris, has fled to Germany. The other journalists have probably had to pack their bags as well, or go into hiding. Marshal Pétain had to abandon his residence in Vichy. According to many people, he was a traitor and he went back with the Germans. We later learned this was true.

The German soldiers are beginning to leave as well. On the rue de Belleville, which crosses the church square and leads to the Porte des Lilas, I

watch as cars, motorcycles, and trucks pass chaotically. The soldiers look tired and scared. They are either old or very young, about the age of my friends' big brothers. They are poorly dressed and their uniforms seem to have been hastily buttoned.

A Mercedes convertible with a flat tire comes clanking down the street. Everyone jeers and yells insults. A grey front-wheel-drive Citroën bearing a French flag passes quickly in the other direction. Then the people start shouting, "Put up barricades!" Boards, pieces of furniture, and mattresses are piled at the entrance to the church square to block the passage. The first German truck that tries to pass is forced to stop. A few people spit on the soldiers. Some try to beat them. The truck knocks down the barricade and passes through.

Among the crowd, I see two men with blue, white, and red arm bands marked with the letters FFI, which stands for Forces françaises de l'intérieur (Internal French Forces). One man is holding a revolver, another a hunting rifle, but I'm not sure whether they are true Resistance fighters.

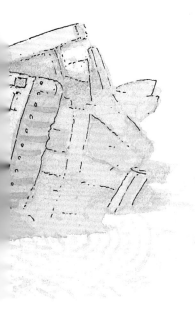

The battle of Paris

August 24. Not all the Germans are leaving Paris. Some have decided to fight. We hear machine-gun shots, explosions, and cannon fire. A new radio station has replaced Radio-Paris, called French Radiodiffusion. On it we learn that the FFI are fighting to extricate the last units of the German army that don't want to surrender. Some serious fighting occurs at the place de la République, not far from our home, where a German barracks is located, and even closer, at the Buttes Chaumont.

In the afternoon a rumor spreads that the first Allied soldiers have entered Paris! Frenchmen from the division of General Leclerc supposedly have arrived at city hall. Because the radio has been cut off, no one knows anything more.

That night I run into Jean Beaudry, who lives across the street. His aunt and uncle are concierges of an apartment building on the other side of the Buttes. This morning, they heard people running, gunshots, then someone knocking on the door of their building. "Please, let me in, I beg of you! Open up!" They were so afraid they did nothing. They heard another gunshot, a muffled sound, and then silence. They waited for everything to grow calm before opening the door. A young man was lying dead on the sidewalk. An FFI. They learned that he was twenty-two years old, that he was born in Warsaw, Poland. Most likely he was Jewish and was fighting against the Germans. Jean Beaudry's aunt and uncle felt a little ashamed.

Now it is night. It must be ten o'clock. Everything is calm; the streets are completely dark. Suddenly all the church bells begin ringing, louder and louder and at top speed, including ours, of course. What a wonderful racket! Everyone understands from this that Paris has been liberated. We light candles in the windows and go down to the street. Everyone is kissing and hugging.

The first jeep

August 25. The occupation of Paris is over! The Americans are here! All my friends and I want to do is see what they look like. We take off on foot-Beaudry, Naudinat, and I-because the metro still isn't working. We walk straight ahead, figuring that we'll surely end up running into them. The morning is already warm, and the weather is still pleasant. The streets are deserted.

In the distance we finally see a small group gathered around a military car, in the shade of some trees near an intersection. Four American soldiers are sitting in a jeep. We approach, very impressed. They smile at us and we shake their hands. Other children come near, too. Young girls throw their arms around their necks and kiss them. They give us pieces of chewing gum-the first I've ever seen-and some chocolate. They are wearing uniforms but don't have boots, sword belts, or any of the other warlike accessories the Germans had. All four are wearing the same type of

shirt, and yet one of them must be an officer, because
he has three little stripes painted on his helmet. I look
at the jeep. It has no doors, which must make it easier
to get in and out of, but it is equipped with everything else one might need: shovels on the side, a winch
in the front, and a big barrel of reserve gasoline
attached to the back, near the spare tire. On the hood
is the American army emblem, the stencil of a big
white star. It strikes us as being very friendly.

Paris reawakens

The streets quickly grow lively again. The merchants open their stores even though there isn't much to sell. We see flags in windows everywhere~American, British, and, of course, French. I wonder how people could have made them so quickly. The fighting has stopped, yet once in a while a few gunshots sound, causing passersby to take cover in doorways. They come from people with guns hidden in the top-floor rooms, under their roofs. People say they're "collaborators" shooting their last bullets randomly on the crowd to get revenge for having lost the war.

A woman is dragged to the church square and seated on a chair. She is practically naked. People insult her and spit at her. A man shaves her head completely with clippers. The crowd laughs. She is accused of having had a German officer as a boyfriend, who of course is no longer here to defend her.

We discover that there were real Resistance fighters among the people in the neighborhood, such as Mr. Bertinot, whom we saw every Sunday at church as if nothing out of the ordinary were happening, even though he was an officer in a secret network. His wife and two children didn't even know!

In our building, the woman on the sixth floor really was hiding an aviator, a Canadian. But it is difficult to learn more, as she still doesn't talk much.

On the rue Faubourg du Temple, alongside the building that served as a German army barracks, right before the place de la République, are two mounds of earth that extend past the sidewalk and are marked with pieces of wood in the shape of a cross. They say that two German soldiers were buried there by their comrades.

The general is here

August 26. General de Gaulle has arrived in Paris! He marched down the Champs-Elysées all the way to the place de la Concorde, then went to Notre-Dame Cathedral to attend a Mass to thank God. As we were listening to the coverage on the radio we heard gunshots! The reporter screamed, as did everyone else inside the cathedral, judging by the cries that reached us through the loudspeaker. Apparently everyone fell to the floor, except for the general, who remained proudly standing.

Newspapers are being published again. But of course they're no longer the same ones. *Le Petit Parisien* is now called *Le Parisien libéré*. Instead of *Paris-soir*, we have *Défense de la France*, which a few days later becomes *France-soir*. There is also *Combat* and *Le Populaire*. While the new titles sometimes resemble

the old ones, the journalists are new. Many of them are the same ones whose voices we heard on the BBC, the radio in London. Those who collaborated with the Germans have fled or are in prison. My father doesn't know which newspaper to choose yet, so for now he tries them all, except for *l' Humanité* and *Franc-tireur*, which are Communist.

Thanks to the newspaper photographs and to cinema newsreels, we are finally able to see what General de Gaulle looks like. (Before the Liberation we only saw photographs of German generals.) He is very tall. You can always see his cap above the crowd and his big arms making a "V" for victory.

The illustrator Jean Effel drew a picture of the Eiffel Tower embracing General de Gaulle. He made them the same size!

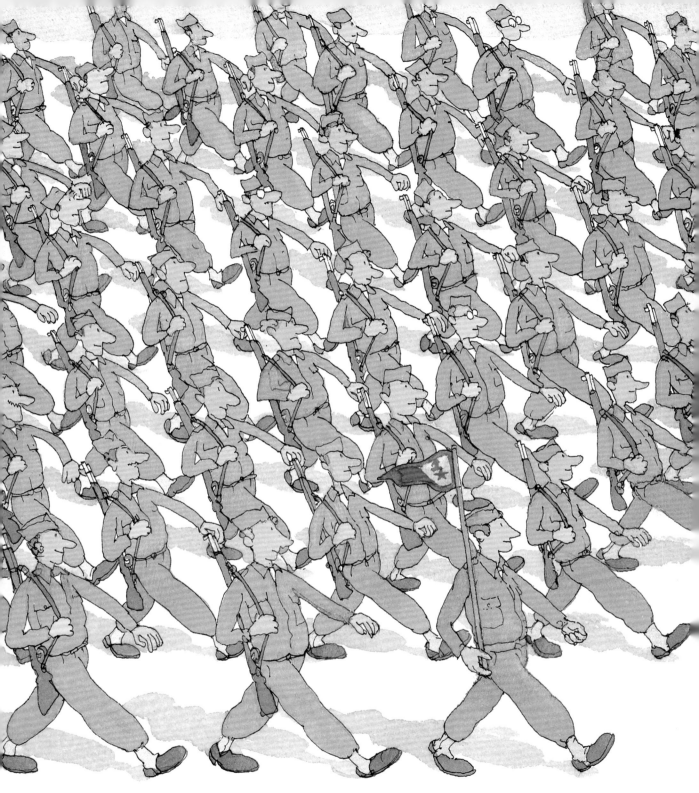

Strike up the band

Today, Sunday, there is a big American army parade on the boulevard, with
trumpets, tubas, trombones, and drums. The marchers are all wearing

soft-soled shoes, even the officers. You can barely hear the sound of their steps above the music, just the slipping of rubber soles. It seems more like an athletic parade than a military one.

Back to school

October. I'm back with my fellow students and professors at Voltaire High School. Fräulein Grün, the singing professor, is gone. Some say she fled to Germany. For us, the green of her clothing was manifestation of her penchant for the Germans. Or perhaps she had her head shaved, or was shot, as some people believe.

Once again we are studying a second foreign language. This time everyone chooses English, without exception. Our teacher is wonderful; he's a captain in the American army and comes to school in uniform. When I stand up to answer a question, I try to imitate his pronunciation as best I can. Everyone in the class laughs at this, which makes me mad.

The Americans show us many interesting things. The Reynolds ballpoint pen, for example, which has ink that sometimes blots on the paper but which can write under water. The women are talking about nylon stockings, which don't run and are supposedly much more durable than the silk stockings from before the war. There is also DDT powder, which is incredibly convenient for getting rid of fleas and lice.

My friends and I often go to the Bois de Vincennes, a park, where all sorts of debris from the American army is heaped up in an enclosure. We gather sticks of black powder about as big as a pencil, but hollow. We don't know what they're used for, but if you put them in an empty aspirin tube and light them, they turn into rockets that shoot across the street and make lots of smoke.

The cinemas are now showing American films, with stars my mother used to tell me about–Gary Cooper, Myrna Loy, Fred Astaire, and others no one knew about, like Cary Grant, Deanna Durbin, and especially Veronica Lake, whose right eye is always hidden under a lock of hair. All the girls want to wear their hair like her. My parents forbid my sister from doing it; they say it will harm her vision. But the war isn't over. The fighting continues. The French provinces of Alsace and Lorraine are not yet liberated. Jojo, our Belgian friend on the second floor who helped us make false food tickets, decides to enlist. He just turned twenty. He is going to join the first French army of General de Lattre de Tassigny. I would have preferred that he enlist in General Leclerc's famous armored division.

1945. The fighting is now taking place in Germany. The end of the war is near. The Russians enter Berlin first. It is announced that Hitler committed suicide with poison. But since his body was burned, many people think it was a final trick–that he isn't dead and will reappear one day. However, his dentist delivers a definitive verdict: He recognizes Hitler's teeth. But since he's also German, he might not be telling the truth . . .

The entire world discovers what happened to the deported Jews and everyone else the Germans arrested. These people were brought to camps, surrounded by barbed wire, in Büchenwald, Dachau, and Auschwitz. Those who are still living are just skin and bones; all the others perished–gassed, burned and carbonized in crematoriums. The newsreels show us terrible, horrifying images.

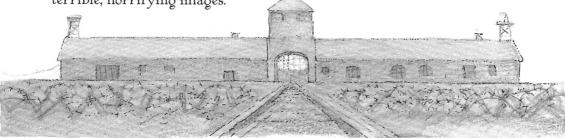

The war is over

This summer we all return to Vitré. I am now twelve years old. Uncle Albert got his car back in working order, a big front-wheel-drive family car he had hidden in a shed. Normandy is not very far and we decide to visit the landing beaches. Bernières with the sea lice, Langrunes, Courceuilles, Saint-Aubin, and then Blonville, which we left behind in 1939 when war was declared. The entire coast is devastated; the Atlantic wall is nothing but a pile of collapsing concrete blocks. All that's left of Uncle Eugène's lovely villa on top of the hill, with its beautiful view, is a white bathtub with lion's paws at the bottom of a giant shell-hole full of rubbish. A bomb fell right in the middle of the house.

Avranches, Bayeux, Caen, and other cities and villages of Normandy are in equally bad shape. People stroll in the sun along streets lined with bombed-out buildings, murmuring, "Here there was a grocery store, there a café . . ."

The newsreels also show us German cities–Hamburg, Stuttgart,

Cologne, Dresden and of course Berlin–where the bombings killed hundreds of thousands of people. Everything has been destroyed. Only ruins are left, as far as the eye can see.

On the other side of the world, Japan continues to fight. Until August 6. On that day, we learn that the Americans dropped a bomb on Hiroshima; it was only one bomb but it was a new kind, which in an instant destroyed the entire city and killed over a hundred thousand people. Three days later, a second atomic bomb–that's the name of this new weapon–is dropped on Nagasaki. The Japanese surrender.

On September 2, the Second World War ends, almost six years to the day after the French and English entered the war against Germany.

October. It's the first time we go back to school in peacetime. We still have to use ration tickets. Many things are lacking, but we no longer eat rutabagas and Paris has light again. My father has chosen a newspaper; he decided on *Le Figaro*, which he was reading even before the war. He's still a drawing teacher. He hopes to be able to do another book, but the first one didn't earn enough money to pay for a second. My mother still works hard to feed us three times a day. My sister is a good student; she would like to continue her studies but Papa says she has to work, so she's taking secretarial courses. We never saw Miss Rosenthal, her piano teacher, again.

Now I'm in ninth grade at Voltaire High; the baccalaureate exam is in two years. In my class, one student came back from being deported. He was arrested in 1942 during the big roundup of the Jews. We all stand around him, full of admiration but frightened when he tells us what he went through–the cold, the hunger, the rats, and the kapos, prisoners chosen by the Germans to survey the other prisoners and who were worse than the guards themselves. And the constant death all around him. He says he weighed 61 pounds when he returned. His parents and two sisters never came back.

He's the hero of the class. For him, as well, the war is over.

Permissions Department, Harcourt Brace & Company,

6277 Sea Harbor Drive, Orlando, Florida 32887-6777.

Creative Editions is an imprint of The Creative Company,

123 South Broad Street, Mankato, Minnesota 56001.

Library of Congress Cataloging-in-Publication Data

Besson, Jean-Louis. October 45: childhood memories of the war/

written and illustrated by Jean-Louis Besson: Translated by Carol Volk.

ISBN 0-15-200955-8

1. Besson, Jean-Louis–Diaries–Juvenile literature. 2. World War, 1939-1945

Personal narratives, French–Juvenile literature. 3. World War, 1939-1945

France–Juvenile literature. 4. Children–France–Diaries–Juvenile literature.

1. Besson, Jean-Louis. 2. World War, 1939-1945–Personal narratives, French.

3. World War, 1939-1945–France. 4. Diaries. I Title.

D802.F8B463 1995   940.54'8144-dc20 94-34544

Printed in Italy   First edition A B C D E

Designed by Rita Marshall